S W E E

Other books by John Barton

A Poor Photographer

Hidden Structure

West of Darkness: a Portrait of Emily Carr

Great Men

Notes Toward a Family Tree

Designs from the Interior

Destinations, Leaving the Map

SWEET ELLIPSIS

John Barton

ECW PRESS

CANADIAN CATALOGUING IN PUBLICATION DATA

Barton, John, 1957-
Sweet ellipsis

Poems.
ISBN 1-55022-354-2

I. Title.

PS8553.A78S93 1998 C811'54 C98-930258-X
PR9199.3.B36S93 1998

Edited for the press by Michael Holmes.

Cover photo: Lilienthal Glider, 1895. Prints and Photographs Division, The Library of Congress.

Author photo by David Young.

Design and imaging by ECW Type & Art, Oakville, Ontario.
Printed by AGMV Marquis Imprimeur, Cap-Saint-Ignace, Quebec.

Distributed in Canada by General Distribution Services,
30 Lesmill Road, Don Mills, Ontario M3B 2T6.

Published by ECW PRESS,
2120 Queen Street East, Suite 200,
Toronto, Ontario M4E 1E2.
www.ecw.ca/press

for Jim and Neile

and

in memory of Charles Cooper and Robin Skelton

for Vicky,

with best wishes,

Ongoingness, vanishing: the world's twin poles.
Heaven's Coast, Mark Doty

It was so easy for a poem to be fraudulent, for what was
the difference, really, between an ellipsis and a vacuum?
Swann, Carol Shields

TABLE OF CONTENTS

Dementia

Objectivity

White Space

Centre of the World

DEMENTIA

PUSHING UPSTREAM

Below my window, men in boats
are blasting a way into the river, moving

up from the mouth,
slowly, charge by charge,
                                        exploding the myth
winter suspends over the current,

ice thick and green enough to bear my weight.

I wanted to believe in its permanence,
an opaque
body stretched out on its stomach, a man fast asleep,

sealing in the sweet
stagnant rancour of fish-spawn and riverweed,
frogs dropped like cold stones
to the riverbottom, flesh made ice.

But the men below my window are insistent,
blasting a way in,
making room for orange
motorboats, blasting caps and life-jackets,

boys at play in the snow-melt, inducing the thaw.

Their bodies sweat, give
shape to loose clothing as they kneel,
tap in another charge
just far enough from the edge.

I wanted to believe in the ice,
no matter how thin and cold,

and now I must live with
the gap between
each explosion and its shattering report,

men silently running well back of the spray
of ice shards
and the approaching

open: the man

with the lithe body who once
fell asleep in my bed,

how he could never give enough
to me, except his own
guilt, not even the chance
intemperate spasm of his penis's flume.

And now I must live with
the aftershocks, the immediate

shuddering cracks in this love I have for him;

how they flash

through his absence with the presence
of another, of anyone
who explodes this layered

green myth: you, lucky
fellow
in a motorboat, pushing upstream.

UNDERCURRENT

This is a bad semaphore
we practise
under the trees in the darkness, the damp white flags

of our t-shirts unable
to tease out

surrender as we move toward and away and past

one another, eyes
hungrily averted as we

pause

feet apart somewhere downstream along this
bridle path by the river,
the invisible

sibilant undercurrent deafened
by the cicada roar —
electric

morse code charging
the humid air of the city,
singing the *long*, *long*, ecstatic *short*

circuit of desire, the physiologic

imperative to be spent,
to be filled,

the white of our t-shirt dampness

impotent in the moonlight,
stained by pollen loose on the breeze,

what we want
not meant by the language

we tease out with flags,
its indefinite

pronouns not about the long
first person singulars of our cocks,
intimacy

straining against cotton shorts,
this language
the only language of love

available, though it does not include
us as *we*,
though we use it

badly, the damp t-shirt whiteness,
the fraternal tanned
presence underneath smelling of river algae and sweat

not drawing us closer,
our fear of how the white

flags of language distort

our kinship, seal us in the airless
eternal privacy of *they*

at the bottom of the river, graveyard of lovers

who unlike us, beloved stranger
(the park signs want us to believe)

could not resist the vortex.

AUTOPSY

What was said:
the official story.

What was said

in *The Edmonton Journal*,
about a boy with beautiful hands.

Who played piano.
A base brat. A nomad.

Who — 6′ tall and suddenly good-
looking — dissipated
his virginity early, at Lahr in Germany (*Bobby*),

who could have been

a model (someone said)
or an actor
larger-than-life and working in Hollywood.

Who was redeployed back
home with his family,
displaced from the known by the end

of a Cold War
that was habit-forming,
the base closures long overdue.

Who found himself

in St. Albert, which the Oblates
built outside Edmonton,
a wind-chilled suburb of heaven on earth.

Who was disoriented

by yet another school,
the student body too upmarket

to revel in Nirvana,

Kurt Cobain shaking down
the house while his father worked yet
another base, the hushed
tree-lined streets around their unfamiliar

split-level coiling
anxiety into the sparse Alberta scrub.

Who hung out at the Boystown Café
and may have (unofficially)
lost his (virginity)
yet again, at 17, this time with a (man).

Who was cool

and getting cooler.
Who seemed
restless and to his mother

solitary,

who ate badly, returned fewer
calls from his friends, who cried

the day Cobain died
by his own hand,
the left side of his face blown away, the outraged

feedback of his guitar unplugged
and shut
forever into the silence

of its battered case,
a generation closed out.

Stupid and contagious —

scrawled into Bobby's diary, its pages black
and blue
with copycat poems.

Who logged his abandonment

into the virtual, looking for someone,
'Nirvana' his password.

Who graduated from the last
of many high schools, the official ones.

Who a week later snuffed nights
of unofficial
hell without Kurt — *Canada*
Day — more than Bobby's eardrums blown out

by Nirvana and Cobain's enticing
growl on endless
replay when he was found

by a sister, remaining
eye open, left
side of his face a mask torn away

from an unenlightening blankness.

Who helped him?
Who helped whom?

Someone had to (someone said) — the body
in Bobby's bed not
a sick joke or a special effect.

(*Bobby*)

who his parents can't stop
praying for,
their only son not born again.

Premature rest — and eternal.
What was said.
Kurt Cobain. Nirvana.
The official story. Bobby's beautiful hands.

BEYOND RECOGNITION

Something reverses
and the blown

apart bits   of last night

        fly back into   place.
Your hands reattach

with the nerves of the wrist,
the energy

of fingers holding a recurrent
cigarette as it burns

hole after hole through the air,
explosiveness

never quite able to

tear free of your buttoned
silk shirt,
though it wants to,
such sudden red luminescence

blinds me at the prospect,

rubble all around us,
the ruined lives of other men

in the bar burned
beyond
recognition by love's nitro

is how I might have remembered you,

eyes rinsed with scotch, anxious
and bloodshot,
not ready for me to tongue them shut,

for the intimacy
of another little death.

LOOSESTRIFE

A solitary bumblebee loud as a far-off
speedboat on the river moves up
the shaft

of loosestrife,
lingers inside each invasive
magenta trumpet cacophonous against the sun, the ecstatic

furred blur of thorax and wings scattering
the premature heat of morning
as we rise up

stairs abandoned to
progressive rust, flakes of it caked
into my lifeline, the river clear as oxygen,

your boat at anchor, the leaking wooden
dingy we left on the shingle
pulled well above

currents eager to shoulder
dead weight beyond the impasse of rapids.
Last night, in the sudden coolness, I was inside

a man deeper than I thought possible,
up to the hilt while your cock
pressed against my spine,

three bodies
rocked together and apart
by stars snared in the riverweeds,

our sweat flamed by a moon only a plunge
into black unconsciousness
could extinguish,

an instinctual need
for breath exploding back through the surface,
our three heads buoys of light in some unnamed constellation.

Your lover drifts with the boat in and out
of sleep while we follow
the trace

of an osprey through
the transparent, a fish in its talons, predatory
circles lowering toward something high in the branches.

Loosestrife chokes the river margins below,
the solitude of bumblebees
complicit

in its spread.
Though you held me in your arms
last night, rocked me ever deeper into the ecstasy

of the man you love, his hungry flesh opening to mine,
I lay my head back against your chest
and gave up nothing.

DEMENTIA

The blood that stagnant,
sometimes sudden

river,
fast-moving and virulent.

Stories, currents
rising all too often to the wrists.

Why else do we slit them,
gorgeous, delirious.

Anger subletting the body,
flaring, uneasy

blood engorging organs.
These days we wear

protection, like raincoats,
an impermeable

layer of skin against the storm
within, two men gowned

like doctors in this way only
for an operation,

this bed,
the stories we don't want shared,

we can't stand them,
their dénouement clinical solitude.

We are careful with each other.
The unsheathed

penis
a conduit of the loose-tongued

dementia we have come to be
afraid of, stories

leaking from the bloodstream,
my love, your love

confused with hurricanes
shouldering inland

from the coast,
the dawn birds silent,

flash flood and dissipating
mass destruction.

New paths for all rivers,
our destinies never the same.

NUMBER THEORY

Far out into orbit,

the satellite's been launched,
launched from the cargo bay, spinning

not quite from
between
the thighs of the astronaut but remotely

programmed by touch,
the keyboard extending its reach with the robotic
arm.
The satellite spinning away —

solar panels opening like

wings —

It receives at last and in a thousand languages

transmits
the first signals at an altitude far

beyond what we can see, except at night.
We follow the thread

of its faint

revolution without binoculars through rips

in the indigo stratus above

this planet where you and I
on a balcony know

no more than each other's names.
Which seem
to represent us whether they are accurate or not,
which we answer to,

like Soyus or Anik.

Tonight, over dinner, something unnamed
was served,
the savour uncertain

out of this world, piquant

like the salad of strawberries and freshly
milled pepper on spinach,
its structure more delicate

than gallium arsenide

devices.

Not quite known to us, as enticing

as quasars — star-like
red presences
at the edge of the universe proven

so far only in theory by numbers relayed
from the satellites wheeling,
data gathered
with the Hubble telescope a fraction

of some primary

whole,

circumstantial evidence
reconfigured on earth for our benefit

pixel by pixel.

A potted
history of the big bang
some men reset the hands of two
hearts by,

by virtue of a faint
subatomic hunger

for touch;
two
bodies of light beyond the visible

spectrum timelessly roaming the celestial vacuum.

TOUCH-SCREEN

Welcome to my museum;
I am its artifact,

rescued by a curator with a good
eye from the backlog.
I bear an accession number,

not the old kind

tatooed on the wrist, but one stamped
into a cracked S.I.N.
card tucked in my wallet.

To anyone
unsure of what I am

here to represent,
my exhibit label points out how
characteristically tight

these faded jeans fit,
conforming

to my hips from an afternoon
of lying
stoned in the bathtub while some mother
whines at the door,

just another typical mendacious and lazy
long-haired child of the 70s.
The past

piles up everywhere —

quadraphonic sound, black light
posters, love beads,
earth shoes with negative
heels — undescribable by the usual

tags.
Besides, who reads?
The narrative is touch-screen,

these ribs.
And my penis: pure living

history hanging representatively out
of sight for as long
as I can remember, the first

interactive, now retrievable
and on display
at the whim of the visitor.

Today it is more than ever
responsive to touch.

I am a demonstration, every gesture nothing
less than semiotics, vicarious orgasm.
Watching the monitor mounted
on my neck

in place of my head, anyone

can scale the erotic
mountains
of my youth with pitons and rope, set

the speed of the stored

full-motion video — pure pornography — and climb
a rockface to the rear
of a comely
unselfconscious guide, his hard

breathing and curses whispered through snug
headphones, the audio
flirtatious, leading all the way

to the summit, the legs

of the Bow Valley spread wide

far below,
the Vermilion Lakes pink as skin
coursing in time-lapse through channels where moose
feed at twilight.

Technology allows the viewer
to zoom in or pull back.

And the sky,
whether it is real or not,

is the limit.

TANTRUM

Moments we've spent alone
could fill one hand.
The most recent passed
by the ocean on a bad day;
my blood was full of storm.

No one has ever understood
this weather, Father,
you are not alone.
Something crests inside,
long swells that build
up and crash at last

and fall, its wash a legend
across the wetlands,
the salty random
feel of it, an undertow
not giving up the dead,
a boy's small body,

my rage, not ready to
leave the water,
back arched
against the dank
slippery change-room floor,
legs kicking, holes
torn out of a steamy
silence of naked
men before their rotten
wooden lockers, eyes
averted, the amazement

you hurled afterward into
my mother's eyes, the hushed
accusations you were forced
up against, as she turned away.
He's my son! You let her
blame you for everything.
I was two years old,

loved the warm embrace
of lulling waters —
leave me be! —
knowing nothing of what could
and could not be healed.
By then you knew,
knew every aching curve
beyond the viewpoint,

descending Sulphur Mountain
from the Upper Hot Springs,
1959, our cold lunch
eaten in a shelter
by some sluggish river,
the corpse-like current
dancing in the drizzle's
somnambulant tracer fire.

You kept your distance,
named it loyalty.
Loyalty the only stone
left for your defence
sinking beyond reach

through the algae-mired
mirror of an untroubled
surface, stillness
around which something
living was firmly tied.

HOMOEROTICISM

What frightened you
as we wrestled, a small boy
and his father, your body pushing me away?

Even as I reached for you, an ordinary man I had yet to learn
the feel of, mystery ached behind your cream
shirt buttoned snugly

at the neck and wrists;
my bare feet snagged in the cuff
of your left trouser-leg; a knee-up toppled me

into your arms, your legs akimbo as I flipped face
down into the responsive spring
of the sofa, the shrill

chords of my laughter
damped like the sticky keys
of the out-of-tune piano you never let me play.

Music is what came to divide us, separates us even now.
In the kitchen my mother gritted her teeth
while on the radio something

called a symphony (how she hated them)
raced up something you called
a crescendo — you

and I spent at last on the floor,
those strings losing all their hysteria
and sudden feline speed. While we lay panting

my mother scooped moist balls of melon into a bowl,
sweet honeydew tickling my nostrils
as I reached for you,

a small boy with quick fingers
at your belt. Something I had no name for
made me want to touch you, your strange body, find out

if under our clothes and elsewhere we were the same.
Even today I hear the muscular
verve of the music fading

from our ears that night.
Red-faced, you stood up and turned off
the radio and straightened your clothes. What frightened you?

Like the hesitant men I am drawn to, I could have
loved you, your arms folded against my small
perfect body as you pushed me away.

II

What have I forgotten?
Who are you? What did I want
from you so long ago? Were you the man

I watched urinate, to my boy's eyes your penis
so large and luxurious and alarming —
so different from mine,

a scrap of wet and loose
hanging flesh that scared me, a tiny
Swiss-army knife missing one or two gizmos?

Someone was always telling me to keep it
to myself, untouchable and unloved,
not the sensitive

gay blade it's grown into.
I can't show you (it is not polite
to point). No one wants to see my beautiful toy.

What was I doing in the bathroom with you?
Were we feeding the goldfish?
Was it lunch time?

Did I need to go pee?
Did I wash my hands afterward? Who are you?
Did I want to kiss you, touch you, bring you inside me?

III

Was I to be one of the girls then,
one of the daughters? Or would you have
preferred a teen-age half-back with the appropriate swagger?

Zip up my strapless formal or lend me your athletic support.
Be supportive. Remember fantasy involves quick
costume changes, lights, the usual magic.

The boys on the football team who laughed
at how badly I kicked might have found themselves
suddenly naked and scoring touchdowns in the Antarctic,

if I had my way, before they froze stiff. Was I afraid
to love them, such thighs and Olympian chests;
I would have liked to enslave them,

their sweats for me alone to strip off.
The only way I could do so was to put on Mother's dress.
I have tried to get by with these sexist crinolines ever since.

Fuck it, Daddy; whose fantasy is this anyway?
I am who I am. Don't touch the music.
Isn't it time you undressed?

IV

I will sleep with you one last time,
Father, though it is not you I hold in my arms.
This man embodies your distance, which I mistook for charm.

I love him, of course, and of course, I love you.
But this is the last time we will sleep
together because he is afraid

of my body, the pleasure it gives him.
He is afraid to take my cock in his mouth;
he is afraid of his own darkness and the cut on my lip.

Father, when I was small did I ever sneak
into bed with you, did I ever steal
some of your warmth?

This man in my arms tonight, he smells
thievery in my sweat; like you he nervously hums.
Father, this will be the last time I will sleep with you,

but I ask for your blessing. Father, love me,
give me the courage to love back.
Give me the desire

to rise from this
bed unafraid of the chance
and expectant man who I know will someday hold me

in his arms without fear. May his tenderness
ease up inside me, may the music of my
warm body stay with him forever.

CONFIDENTIAL

When I bent
to pick, my hands
came away red and wet
Margaret Atwood

In blood we trust, its integrity
channelled, a power grid

of veins,
those neutral carriers.

What is tested and pronounced clean.
What we want not always kept within

the speed limit, the streamlined
body dripping with desire,

sodden with such honesty, rosy
and watered

as well-tended garden soil.
Leaning on the rakes, our bodies

both contained and containing
worlds governed by something

internal, not merely mutual
rules of the road,

but an impulse rising
above the genetic,

above that surgical by-pass
of the city where we find

ourselves living no matter what
wildernesses lie

beyond the civic boundaries,
though one or two of us

still have the confidence to subsist
from the land, raise

our own strawberries, which bleed — so she
said: a blood instinct

for survival (and strawberries) on our own terms.
Such heartiness

fortunate and outside the ever waning
listening area of the CBC,

its signal weakened, information
a newsroom virus.

In blood we trust,
only now to distrust.

Prejudice leaking into the stream
of conscience

no longer containable by our veins,
the garden flooding with intent.

Do not name us
and our blood will testify

at your inquiry,
establish who has blood on whose hands

no matter how we were swept off
course, our cars

carried from the freeway
and much farther

downstream toward our final destination
than any of us had planned,

with no chance for factory recall
since nature has acted.

And do not blame us
because we have

lost the freedom to bleed,
those among us who cling to uprooted

trees and hydroelectric pylons,
the cut lines

snakes cinched about us, bleeding
venom and fire, our futures

dangerous, outside the reach
of the sharp grappling

hooks of your half-hearted
rescue boats, our consanguinity

in doubt — just like
the others who slipped free

of their seatbelts while no one
was looking, only to become

trapped bloodlessly underwater
in rapidly leaking

interiors of air, those vacuums.
Take us

into your confidence.
We are innocents, every one

of us (*in blood we trust*), and like you
betrayed, the credulous

love of the earth still larded
under our bruised

and ragged
nails.

MISSISSIPPI

How to interpret what is current
between us,
the electric slough at twilight, the symbols

keyed into memory and then with such
impulse one gentle and
solitary
<*cr*> sends so

much across emptiness, a power surge,
a flood,

the characters,

the character magnetic, attracting our fingers,
which we entwine in the act

of input, the flesh fibre-optic,
charged with an ether

net of nerves,

the ditch I cross beside the parkway exit ramp
each morning, half-moon-shaped,
(my lop-
sided heart thinking out loud, nervous

for responses: yours,

mine, anyone else who listens in) a truncated

bit/memory byte of river
tremulous with ooze,
an oxbow

humming with midges and bulrushes and golden
rod and all other
imaginable virus, longing a fever

a delirium between

men, you and I: this love, this virtual
noise
at last something

codable, pure static
and amphibious

lyric, tadpoles and the whine of the crickets
deafening as I
walk through marsh grasses on the way in

to dailiness, snagging
the hair on my lower thighs and my hard-wired
routine,
reading the messages

left overnight by the others, sometimes
by you, whose lips

might well be electric, who sends me

hugs,
such voltage, *o love*

in 1993 such fertile wantonness: the Mississippi floods.

DESTINY

September, October —
the leaves shake loose
in stages,
first red then yellow,
mustard-cold bleeding
through the fading rosehip of freefall
maples.
I cross the park early
each morning, the crystal
air bottomless and sharp as kirsch,
the squirrels
cavorting among scattered leaves like disembodied
handlebar mustaches,
tails mimicking the bodies' spritely
balletic curves.

When we make love, why are we so nervous?
Where you touch me mirrors
how, rib by missing
rib,
I move
with lips and tongue down
your chest and between your
legs, balls held inside
my mouth like a pheasant
in the jaws of a golden retriever
after the hunt —
who needs perfection, but
look, no teethmarks.

Curled against each other
last night,
your sphincter slipped down my second
finger like a ring,
                    a moment of calm —
your chest furred
with damp coarse wool,
                              the silky
down of your spread thighs
and calves
            pulled on over the toes
like loose,
seamless stockings.

Before we fell asleep, you sketched
the leaves for me,
all the figures and shades I have ever desired,
                                    amber, vermilion
        lozenges caught falling
between sedimentary
layers of drawing paper settled over your crotch,
impression upon impression
left behind, smeared with our semen that encrypts
a wet and purple record
into the weave of my blue sheets, our fey
chromosomes going down on one
knee again and again
                        like duck hunters at dusk,
camouflaged in the stealthy
darkness among brittle

reeds fringing the crimson lake, the dischargeable
code
        timeless and alive
as the squirrels you pencilled in,
those tricky,
cartoon pictographs.

That you stepped from myth
I have no doubt.
                Stepped from a recurring
childhood dream of lifting up
the veil, hungry
for a kiss, the photographer's flash
about to
          obliterate
the backdrop,
              its wind golden with falling
leaves,
the icy lace crisp with static
as I throw it back,
                only to find myself
no longer mystified, and married
to a bride
with Chaplin's mustache.

LAKE HURON VARIATIONS

I

Is this the real world?

Pale yellow

brick farmhouses unarticulated
like box cars along
backroads (Highway 7) from Stratford west to Lake Huron —

St. Mary's, Elginfield, Ailsa Craig, Parkhill, Thedford —

late July, corn

fields ripening in the wind, blurring in my peripheral

vision, sunflowers

wheeling as we drive by, Queen Anne's Lace
hanging above
ditches, parachutes open

until the end,

or at least until the end of the season.
Harvest.
Dimensionless

afternoon sunshine and unapparent

co-axial cables linking the houses, eternal touch-

tone phones, receivers crooked
in the hollow
between shoulder and neck, the exchange

of rural news between housewives or farmhands not heard

on the radio
while we drive by

listening to Loreena McKennitt, our Lady of Shalott lyrically
suicidal and drifting downstream as we would

célibataire

toward Camelot past the centre of corrections, the county
hospital, the blunted gothic

steeple of a church I call
St. Sebastian's, friends not lovers (news

not heard on the phone or read
on the society page of *The Stratford Beacon-Herald* before
Long Day's Journey into Night,

but felt,

the love we might have allegedly shared
still inexpressible by most
and sinful,

criminal, sick, a rumour

on the party line between farmhands,
between men) driving

by, one of us

real and one of us not (who and to whom)

rumours floating about us with the goldenrod,
primordial,

our powers of observation conditional
and conditioned,
making hay or not of the farms as we drive by,

of the farmhands,

barechested and golden and sweat-slick

in the sun, ready
for harvest, cellular

phones clipped to their overalls, shoulders
leaning against haystacks that ache

to unroll beneath them,
sweet-smelling mattresses,

ephemera we observe with a passion
and dispassion

that is mine, that is yours —

Which is more real?

II

Freed

of the car radio, of the rumours
and lack of real
news, we arrive and separate,

célibataire,
you down the beach with your backpack and desire

to explore while I take

to the water: this

lake of reality,
this *lac de réalité* deliciously sun-warm and breezeswept,
a crazy wavy *crise*

de nerfs I slip into easily — the waves

since I turned

eighteen
never quite real, but multiple, so many

waves, so many

fears, wanting to

choose a single state and emerge from
the lake of my
constant unreality into consciousness, alight on some far and

elusive

shore: a final solution or landfall, an
identity, this
queerness and quantum

physics I have finally come to —

but at twenty, I chose

death,
my first attempt.

III

How this *lac de réalité* frightens me,
anxiety unable to work

itself out
of my body as sweat, though I swim,
the lake within me wanting

to join with the lake without, the strenuous
effort of being

alive, labouring for *connexion/connection*,
those farmhands.

Multiple waves of connecting,
sex, friendship, hate

co-existing, asynchronously real and unreal
between the same two people

known to each other for more or less years.

Or minutes: you

walking the beach, examining drift
wood, the sand dunes,
the many endangered species of grass, talking
to strangers spontaneously

or so I want to believe
while I labour

toward the right word, the right
spelling — *connexion/connection* — sweet

incantation as I move

through fantasy/*lac de réalité*/poetry

(*lover, where are you*?)
stroke by panicked and luxuriant stroke.

IV

My first attempt.

In *A Poor Photographer* a poem called "The Ocean:"

> *Though despair is without shore*
> *I continue breathing*
>
> *the swimmer's eye opens*
> *a path through tentacles of shadow the waves cast*

long forgotten words
breaking phosphorescently

nostalgically

ashore while I swim
Lake Huron for the first time,

my silhouette trailing below me, sub-
conscious figure caught in silvery daguerreotype sand.

> *fear an awareness we all must chart*

The bodies of water I used to swim
dwarfed me imaginatively,

the farmhands lost in the imagery.

As in: wet dream.

As in: *célibataire*.

The poem closed aptly:

> *words I remember as I swim blindly*
> *the shoreless channels between*

V

My first attempt.

Rising up through

the allusive, love-algaed

rings of another

language at Collège Universitaire

Saint-Jean, it was taken

from me, pumped out

of my stomach at the University of Alberta

Hospital, then referred

to the Drop-In Clinic at the William

Aberhart Institute of

Psychiatry by an intern who might have been

beautiful,

a farmhand,

if I let myself remember, swim

back through my unconsciousness to that room

of definable emergencies, his finger

stuck unromantically

down my throat,

but all

that swimmingly comes back up

are his words — *you might be*

sexually hung

up, this wanna-be

farmhand not appreciating

the reality of his

prognosis, its significance

as I did, though

I didn't think as I would

now that it might

signify *sexually well*

bung;

this man with the unringed

finger stigmatizing

me instantly and for years

I was multiple

insistently, able to swim

unthinking between shoreless

channels in an ocean so lacking in

reality it unsettled

me, *célibataire* not celebratory, unable

to swallow

pills without

milk, unable to swallow

or hear the deep

call of the

body too few

years before I came

to Huron, water saltless and for

a moment fleetingly

substantial,

heavy water not of the nuclear

bloodline, but of love,

a ring of fire shining above me,

as I swim,

a sphincter or an oesophagus,

holy orifice,

queer

light tentacling the warm sand with desire.

VI

What is more real?

Where we began and begin again
as we get into the car

to drive back, our time at Lake Huron
our own and unshared
and understood or not intimately, rushing

as we are

to catch the first
scene of *Hamlet*, that pouty, dressed-up, and suicidal

imperial farmhand manqué,

the drive back in fast rewind —

Thedford, Parkhill, Ailsa Craig, Elginfield, St. Mary's —

the goldenrod, the sunflowers, the corn, the Queen Anne's Lace,
Loreena McKennitt, and the Lady of Shalott.
Bell Cellular. The party line.
The rumours. The steeples. The yellow brick.
The centre of corrections. The hospital. The haystacks.

Who is more real?

The man of flesh, the man on the phone, the man in the lake.
St. Sebastian. Hamlet. The poor photographer.
Eugene O'Neill. The farmhand.

Multiple and *célibataire*.

You? Me?

Nothing or everything?

These are the questions,
whatever the news, its failure to connect.

To be sensual,
to exist, to believe in existence

we must hold and be held.

Fresh water holding me.

Lake Huron variations.

OBJECTIVITY

BLOODSTREAM

This river keeps changing

its name: Richmond, Wellington, Montreal
Road, the currents
                                        of traffic
building up, crest
in a ruddy
flood of heavy metal and car horns after eroding
minute-long stoplights,

shoot through

the torn-out bus mall
like rapids,
where the homeless and commuters used to
come in
under dirty glass from the rain,

wave after wave

of headlights thrown
upward,

starlight along the tarred course

of Rideau Street —
shade of water, curtain of light —

backwash between the Houses
of Parliament and the *patates frites* of Vanier,

the Centre Block having a facial,
a half-century of exhaust
lifted
with a fine spray of sand from the porous mortar and stone

while further east a psychedelic
leviathan
goldfish looms

behind the graffiti streaked across
a boarded-up window

through which a family must have
awaited the late blooming

apples, the youngest in short pants
practising piano, his faulty notes
lingering on the currents
of humid breeze fingering lace,

now carrying

newsprint and the valent scent
of ginger from the Sitar,
of donuts cooking in fresh grease at Tommy's,

the main street of Canada
barely aware of itself cascading

toward that other river where frogs
bellow among the reeds,

indifferent to the airless
buses shaking the Cummings Bridge to its pilings,
lights going out
on either bank, sleepers at last borne

away by the swirling —

WOLVES

there were several converging
moments of grey   sudden
eyes howling
out of the hungry snow stretched to the exposed
throat of the horizon   the December wind lunging

lunging in cold-blooded
gusts   from the maw of the prairie

as we lay together in the torn
tar-paper warmth of the last
quonset hut   lay together at the edge
of town dreaming
the future   the war just over
the first avenues of a hard
won peace about to go in

the surveyors displacing us
the tangle of our well-spent limbs cleared
back   underbrush   skin
roused by the draft's ice-tipped whistling
dusk's blood-red panes rattling

as we returned to brides we barely knew
and our civilian clothes

under the cover of darkness   the aurora
borealis scouring
the distances   prison camp lights   the snow
noisy and alarming underfoot and this is

when it happened   premonition
of the cold war   teeth
at our insides   coming out of nowhere   out of the snow

moments of grey hungrily separating us
and through the years

we have kept the memory of final
passion   hidden teethmarks   cyphers

scrambled in the headlines
J. Edgar Hoover   Guy Burgess   Roy Cohn
moving in and out of nightmare

with everyone else away from the closed-down
bases at High River and Claresholm

cyphers only we can recognize

on the bus to and from work
in the overrun cities of the plains
the outer limits   unscrolled barbed wire

our sheepish eyes red with the howling
cold wind marauding
from the threatened reaches of the wilderness

DESTINATIONS, LEAVING THE MAP

The map of where you went you left
unfolded on the table,
the Mississippi delta on a bus tour two thousand miles away,
where Edna Pontellier threw herself into the Gulf.

I study the route you marked in felt pen
over the U.S. border into Montana,
the red of secondary roads
through Wyoming and Nebraska blackened by your sure hand.
Even now you are chatting your way across the plains
with balls of wool in the overhead rack,
content with the pensioned freedom
a lifetime of work has bought you
years after the family broke apart,
the continent yours at last
to discover and share,
one arm of the sweater you're making me
equal to a day's conversation
with a retired teacher from Red Deer.

Did you leave this map
in the dining room for me like the key
you left in the milk chute so I could
let myself in after school?
I found notes on the kitchen counter,
Feed the dog.
Shovel the walks before I get home.

Did you forget the map
or did you leave it
open beside the book I am reading
so I would know where you had gone?

As a child I drew maps of countries
found nowhere else but my room.
No one could follow me as I floated down
the twists and turns of every river,
braved deserts and harsh winters,
gave names to mountain ranges and lakes,
compiled notes on the flora.
No one could disturb me while I repaired my canoe.

Stories of the past and future like maps unfold.
While your bus stops for coffee
outside Little Rock (marked in red
boldface beside a star),
a woman at the end of the last century
gives up to the subterfuge
of the sensual, her abandonment
mine as I am pulled along by the current
of narrative in *The Awakening*,
first by the speculative caresses
of a young lover, Edna Pontellier abandoning
her husband and children, abandoning
convention only to be abandoned in love,
the luxuriant, freeing waters
of the Gulf the only choice left
to her besides unhappiness,

the undertow sweeping her far
beyond land, drawing me in
while your bus crosses Louisiana,
a Greyhound carrying women
who may yet survive divorced husbands,
the complaints of daughters and sons.
The long awaited warm waters
of the Gulf ahead
look beautiful through all the waking
stages of the sun as it climbs.

HOME MOVIES, NEW TECHNOLOGY

While NASA prepared for *Eagle's*
descent to the Moon,
we raced each other by raft
to a nameless
island just offshore in Crimson Lake.

For two weeks at Pioneer Ranch
we were crammed, twelve
mismatched boys per cabin, and now
each cabin was a team, each boy paddling
or kicking for speed, the vacuum
of water we dove in and out of
barely colder than blood, pooling
in a cavity the glaciers dug
from the prairie while the Moon
looked placidly on, invisible
behind the white heat of the sky.

The heart in each boy lifted,
sky-high at the prospect
of arriving and returning first,
twelve-year-old explorers going beyond
Cartier, Champlain, Fraser, Mackenzie,
a taste for manifest destiny
and conquest swelling inside us,
a new world where we would be
taller, wiser and mythic.

Handicrafts had kept us back
from adventure all week.
At last we were men racing
toward an island some boy scout
had christened the Moon.
For one afternoon Crimson Lake
was the universe
and we pushed at its limits.
Who we were consumed us.
We forgot the planet was home
to more than just us, though
TV announcers kept harping on
about it hourly — humanity united,
they said, by what was beamed back,
everything larger than life
on a building-high screen
in Nathan Phillips Square.
It would take us years
to realize how many on Earth
at the time knew nothing
of the landing, beyond reach
of more than the air waves,
tilling drought-stricken fields
or in a refugee camp dying.
How many still do not know,
the images yet to reach them
on the wrong side of some border,
in ever worsening fields,
the Moon as we know it
in the night sky no more
and no less in the background?

That all obsessions, however
transitory, must be fulfilled —
a rationale for masturbation, for poetry.
After lights-out we would joke
about the strange machines of our bodies
as they mutated, some of us not yet
literate in their systems
and afraid we would never catch up,
future shock changing everything
too quickly, the talk about girls
and what we would seriously do
with our lives when we grew up
so new and awkward, some of us vaguely
aware of a glitch in the mechanism
of desire that could make us defective,
emotion, intellect, and the body
separating and falling away
in the incremental stages of a rocket.

But this was the last thing
on our minds — or was it? —
when those scratchy home-movies
of the landing lit up the screen
of the dining hall's TV,
Aldrin and Armstrong posing
in real-time with the Earth,
an unearthly sister
modestly smiling between them.

The kitchen staff briefly stopped
serving blue potatoes, red beans,
saffron chicken with green dressing
while everyone watched,
a banquet for space explorers
going cold on our plates,
though I don't remember who won
the race, returned first
from the island.
I was ready to go home,
an alien who wore his brave face
snugly, an astronaut's helmet.

Moon-food we called this feast
and some ate without fear.
Already we sensed the growth
of our bodies was about leaving,
the Solar System and everything
familiar left far behind.
Star-struck, we watched a man
who was both a son and a father
step from the *Eagle*, just as NASA
had planned, into the drained
Sea of Tranquility, ghostly
images of manhood, of danger
vanquished and claimed with a flag.

FROM A JOURNEY AROUND THE WORLD

Consider the crew of able-bodied men
a young boy imagines
taking upriver into the heart
of some continent: Grey Owl,
Jack London, and Joseph Conrad.
Voices drip from your paddle.
As I fall asleep, you sit
cross-legged on the bed,
lips memorizing each
word in the book of voyages —
what to take with you,
what to leave behind —
a pocket flashlight guiding
you into the dark,
the crickets of August in the parched,
noisy rushes along the river
below my window tickling
the cocked ear of a sickle moon.

The *Seniavin* at anchor in Sitka Sound.
You are the nameless
Cossack carrying the samples
Mertens gathers from the mouth
of some uncharted river, the slimy
algae and bladder kelp staining
your uniform with salt,
salt that later sets the ink
preserving a day in the life
of a naturalist and his assistant

documenting Russian-America,
the frontispiece to
Illustrations of Seaweeds
from a Journey around the World
by Decree of Emperor Nicholas I.

How the sun of this new continent
makes your bodies sweat,
layers of the Navy's wool perfumed
with the weight of a three-year voyage.
Look at how perfectly
it stretches across his shoulders.
Whatever story was soaked up
by its tersely woven
fibres is less decipherable than the knotted
records of the Aztecs.

No matter how cold these near Arctic waters,
when the tide comes in,
warmed by the sand and rocks,
how you want to shed all
constraint and swim
with him among the weeds,
sample what can be found in the impressions
your bodies leave in the soft
spongy floor of the river's mouth.

It is dark down here
and in the haze the ship's disappearing
anchor rope gleams, a worm of the sea.
You swim with your eyes open
and your fingers are

blurred specimens under glass.
You can't believe how
easily you turn into this clear element,
yield to the current that feathers
the numberless and lovely
algae releasing oxygen
that the almost prehistoric,
prenatal gills of your body
at last are learning to collect.
You are at home down here,
your skin alive to something
you can't yet put a name to,
Mertens somewhere below or ahead,
your god of the sea,
a father called Neptune.

While I drift toward Atlantis,
you sit on the raft
of my bed with a flashlight,
amazed how the dark face of the deep
appearing so impregnable and endless
from the rolling deck of the ship
from below is now,
for the two of you, a fluttering
wide-open eyelid of sunlight.

CHICKEN BOY

Your mother says you have the pox.
You and she have counted
at least one spongy red spot for every year
carrying you toward the future,
lucky at your age
to put something of the worst
in life behind you, though the virus
may sleep inside your body,
to wake later at some nightmare
point of despair or in old age,
a belt cinched tightly,
breath by breath, into your waist.

Not yet able to imagine
a death that is yours only,
you can't stop talking
about the pox,
how feathers poke up through the skin
spot by spot, a down
with soft pointed spines ripping
who you have been to shreds; at last
the chance to pal around
with Clark Kent when not fighting crime.

My true identity: the desire to be
more than human,
and all to the good.
As a boy I was unaware
of what bitterness I might grow into,
a disease leaving few visible
scars, such weary anger agitating not far
below the skin after
each failure to save and be
saved by
and from the world.

Little Chicken Boy, the earth
keeps growing larger
than I can imagine: CBC NewsWorld profiling
monsters until tonight
less apparent than the dinosaurs.
But why should you care?
Lie down with your moulded plastic sword,
a slain knight already drowsing
in the afterworld.
At the story's end your father
tucks in the covers,
a dishevelled cape of stars.

The house sleeps
and you glide from your window
above the ordinary
streets of your neighbours,
a familiar of the bats and flying squirrels,
the river below a moonlit
serpent with an invisible mouth and tail.
You are something to believe in,
swooping back when everything
is well
to a bed itchy with loose feathers,
the pox fading from your skin.

18 DEGREES NORTH

The last of a night rain
stutters against the tin roof.
Dawn, pink and feathery
with darkness,
lolls up behind coconut palms.

In the back yard a solitary rooster
pauses before the hibiscus,
his cries irritable
as he scratches, strides,
dips back and forth under the fence.

Our window frames him.
Criss-cross of metal fretwork
folds shadows deep
into the folds of our sheets.
Some nights we cross
that narrow space between us,
our bodies pushing
toward oneness until
one crosses back,
our flesh easing asleep,
divided in the splendour
of disorderly twin beds.

The insect whir
of your son's Walkman cuts through
the wall that cuts him from us,
his privacy wound
into a replay of sleep
hermetic with music.
Later the three of us will halve
grapefruits, share coco-bread,
Jamaica unfolding
across the glass table
between us, another day plotted
against the crisp
cartography of mountains and beaches,
our slant toward the island.

Some mornings I work
things out in watercolour,
draw houses across the street,
leave out details,
attempting the whole.
The thick light of sunrise
pours in while I sit
on the doorsill, back turned
to the bare room where you
and he talk, filling in
spaces I cannot.

Once you slept in late.
He sat down beside me,
rubbed the night from his eyes.
He mixed shades
of blue and green for my palette;
flakes of the raw pigments
remain indelible,
a signature
under my thumb nail.

But today he's slept in
and you lounge wordlessly reading.
I withdraw into the shower
and soap down my body,
consoled by the singular
pleasures of touch,
flesh aglow inside
this random envelope of skin.

Every night the moon
through our window
is sharp, tacked low
against the curve of the sky;
a change in latitude draws
some stars more closely
together than we are
used to, pulls
others farther apart.

Some nights we wake to
constellations addled with light.

OBJECTIVITY

A glass of filtered water
poured from a jar stored in the fridge,

drunk leaning against the sink,
cool morning light
transmuting maple leaves caught about the sill,

their shadows tousled, golden
handprints littered across the floor

in a kitchen on Blue Moon Private
near the disused airstrip,
its coordinates beyond empathy,
the tranquility broken only by blackbirds

and a pilot learning to land,
to come gently to

earth in a rented Cessna,
an approach practised repeatedly following
the river down the usual flight path

then, knowing how to separate
and how to return

breaks free, joy-

rides off while, far below, a man
tracks the fading
engine and spreading wings

of sun, sips water, quenching
natural thirsts he's carried all through life,
such desperate cargo

slowly discharged
and unpacked into kitchen cupboards,
bookcases, and the attic,
his belonging

here, in this house, at last comfortably

disposed around him, a proximity
he never felt till now,
watching neighbourhood children set off for school,

balanced on a stool near the window,
the filtered water perspiring

in his hand, its cool perspective,

bottomless, finally equal
to thirsts that have parched him
less since he accepted they will never end,

despite all the scratches, this unbreakable
tumbler kept within reach.

WHITE SPACE

NIGHT OF THE BLUE MOON

In the park where the cemetery
used to be, the dead
reconvene, dispossessed
of their bones, which were removed
beyond the limits of the city.
They set up their instruments
in the fog, the stone
bandstand commanding the unseen
river from the eastern ridge, the lost
Strauss waltz they are
about to play spiritualized,
the acidic quarto no more
than dust in some neglected
corner of the Bibliothèque
nationale in Paris, the violin,
the cello cases open on the wet grass,
the triangle dully gleaming,
Glenn Gould's piano
off to one side, waiting,
the patina slivered
with the fine bones of age,
a dark mackerel sky slanted
into the last pallor of twilight.

They set up their instruments,
room left for dancing later
across the tiles of mica
in evening gloves and spats,
ascots of trailing mist knotted
at the neck, which diamonds

also choke, sudden
stars like ice melting
in glasses at the bar,
melting because no one drinks
any longer, but they fancy
the heaviness of the leaded crystal,
the vodka aesthetic
and preternaturally chilled.

The wind weighs the time
on its hands and settles
in for the night, the flammable
maple leaves not quite
ready to give themselves up
to passion. The dead,
they set up their instruments
and dust the stone parquet
with chalk the sharp
dew will wash away.
Idle fingerings of the board,
the astringent sweep
of horse-hair across tightened
strings while fatigued silks
thread with Kashmiri gold
drag over courtly stone.
Strauss and light untraceable steps,
dawn's rose quartz
a translucent fog resonating
for a long while after,
oxygen disinterrable
like pupa, until it is time
from the manicured and wormy loam.

THE BIT LIKE DESIRE

ride out on some hairy beast,
gallop backward pressing
your buttocks to his withers,
sit to his clumsy gait somehow.
Anne Sexton, 1962.

Anne, you fled on your donkey,
I am happy to say
madness could not throw you off.
You fled to that barren
oasis you saw
as the one possible destination
where you could never grow old.
Somewhere in Appalachia,
fleeing to Egypt like God.

*

It began simply enough,
that last day in Weston,
breakfast early with Louise, watching
chickadees feed outside your kitchen
against October's chill maples.
Then down into Boston
for a session with your shrink
where you left the essentials,
a lighter and cigarettes,
shadowed by a bowl
of flowers on her desk.

Then off to proof
the galleys of what would be
your first, much longed-for
posthumous book,
a last lunch with Maxine,
and home through the clutter
of Indian summer,
the saffrons and the reds,
the car garaged and left
running with the radio on,
Erik Satie and all weather
extinguished,
carbon monoxide blissful,
nullifying as sex.

*

Anne, I have a confession:
I was never your kind,
though I bought your books
in a Minneapolis bookstore one Christmas,
three years after your death,
my own suicide ten months fresh.
All that spring no one knew
how much trouble I took
to practise, with such discipline
swallowed all the ludicrous
red vitamins my mother gave me,
my second year away
from home, to recover my strength.

A week later I had an overdose
pumped from my stomach,
an amateur losing my nerve
as I lay on the narrow
dormitory bed, unable to turn
a deaf ear to the needle
of my record player
hopelessly stuck, a woman
rasping over and over, *I am alive*
but it is the last thing on my mind.

*

Anne, you never faltered,
your voice lives on
as you wished, in books
that are still read,
in academic studies
the living use to secure their names.
Your words remain
on the album you cut.
I blow off the dust
and it plays while I search
files for a poem I wrote
about my death;
your stresses recall
what little I remember,
the narcotic
feel of the rhythms pulsing
through my veins,

metaphor a lift
into the eternal,
some perverse and exalted
space where words tell
us who we are,
you might have said once,
tell us what we have lost,
your mother, your father
in a cemetery outside Boston,
exhumed from the lucid
depths of the subconscious
with a new pair of shoes,
a husband and two daughters,
yet another lover and matching
clutch-bag, a per diem
of words, madness, and fame.

*

Anne, you fled on your donkey.
Not even sanity
could throw you off.
You held onto life to the death,
until language could no longer
speak for you and you freely
let its reins drop,
slackened your hold on the bit
like desire that hauled
you through whatever desert
you chose to recross.

Despite the dryness you never
forgot how the earth
under your nails also breathes
the keenness of shorebirds,
January southeasters,
and love.
Still, you fled on your donkey,
a faithless puritan
on some kind of pilgrimage;
and though the terrible
words you wrote
may yet outlast you
almost twenty years on,
dear Anne, unlike them
you no longer feel pain,
no longer feel the ice
break down into wind-chimes
eroded against each
other in the river-flow
overwhelming the bank
where I pause, the onset
of spring, these razor-edged
shards of jangled
light perpetually singing.

LONE WOLF

I called you the wild child,
a man who had been raised by wolves.
Your body spoke with the mute
language of an animal, gently
and with a caged dignity;
there was a grace
to the anxious, shy
animation of your hands.
The reflective grey-blue
of your watchful, dark-ringed
eyes mirrored back even
the smallest of my movements
as I once made you
supper, a thick broth of root
vegetables and free-range meats
ladled into earthen bowls.
You ate with a delicious,
unselfconscious gusto I came to
love you for on that chill
November night.
A pallid circle of candlelight
shadowed within
the circumference of my table,
brief as a hunter's moon.

You were not the first
animal to trespass
and flee my life, nor were you
to be the last, but few have
left traces so immaculate:
torn, low-slung branches
that only wash against
my face while sleeping,
recurrent unexpected
paw-prints stumbled upon
but disappearing from porous
lake-silt just as I find
myself on the grizzly
haze-lit shoals of morning.

Your skin was furred
with the cool scrubland
air of fall concealing
worked muscle and organs
meant for a life outside
the domestic space you
so often looked in toward
from margins no one could
have guessed the extent of,
your wolfish nature no less
endemic than the genealogies
you knew you would never
carry forward, yet
crouched at the river's edge

as its currents grew less
and less red from dwindling
salmon runs, you may have
felt time drop its restless
weights through your limbs,
its barbed hook waiting
until something wordless
would bite, would quickly
unsex and take your life.

I am sorry it is your death
that has tainted these
words with harvest gold.
I might have spoken
sooner but I had come to
an uneasy impasse
with the civilizing
impotence of what little
language I have to share.
Once I tried to lay
an elaborate and exquisite
trap of desire, its passe-
partout I hoped would
tame you,
tame the quiet anguish
that was your wilderness
and your escape,
a paradise transgressed.

It was only a matter of time
before there were no more
silent places left.
All I ever caught were
your eyes in the roving
headlights of my dumb
and chance affection,
one howling
flash elapsing no longer
than the morse-like
echo of a heartbeat — you blinked
blindly, and I was gone.

THE CRISIS OF LYRICISM

His neighbour frozen before her white
garage door glinting
in the withdrawn Michigan sunlight, a foretaste of snow

Brodsky before us in the classroom
telling stories

the allegory of how he came

to understand Frost as America's foremost
poet of terror, newly
exiled from Russia and teaching in Ann Arbor, this scruffy

brutally sensitive man, ten years later, lounging before us
chainsmoking Marlboros, pausing between haphazard
drags, *Take Five* vented
down through the floorboards from some dimensionless

practice room above...
the national anthem of whatever

united states, it doesn't matter which —
according to Brodsky —
liberty

more or less

an improvisation ever since he first
heard Brubeck jamming
under the stars and sickle moon in Leningrad, the ember

of Joseph's cigarette leading
us toward the blank

face of his argument, a woman
frozen
before her garage

door for almost ten minutes without hoisting it open,
shedding
no light on the clutter within.

I found myself imagining
chainsaws, bicycles, the Toyota
idling in a trance

of exhaust, waiting to be let in,
the garage door blazing against the deluge

of vermilion and harvest, the empty
maples about her, a clutch
of children ready to be taken away by the school bus.

I pictured Brodsky opening his living room
blinds to watch,
the voyeurism that is neighbourliness,

that is art.
For all I know

she cut the demeanour of a mannequin
modelling
slacks at JC Penny, fallen
leaves artfully displayed at her feet, Brodsky watching

her consider what can merely be guessed at,
something stories only can
find words for — "bicycle," perhaps or, "chainsaw,"
the word "Toyota" waiting to be let in.

Or will anyone really believe that?
In today's version
the woman might well hoist the door open, twenty years later is

about to drive in
to humours too private to grasp.
Adjusting the rear-view mirror, who does she

see loitering at the end of her driveway?
If she had any brains
she'd throw the car into reverse without thinking and floor it.

Have I kept her idling against her will?
And what about Brodsky?

Goosefleshed by that cool and stateless
autumn mapped
inside Frost's America

who is able to speak?

SARANAC LAKE VARIATION

I am mainly preoccupied with the world as I experience it,
and at times when I would rather be dead the thought that
I could never write another poem has so far stopped me.
I think this is an ignoble attitude. I would rather die
for love, but I haven't.
Frank O'Hara, September 1959

Boxing Day 1993,
alone in my hotel room, reading
City Poet in the bath (Bruce calls it
Brad Gooch's *I-do-this-I-do-that* life
and times of Frank O'Hara),
water hot and replenishible to my armpits,
toe blocking the overflow,
and I think of you,
far away in New Brunswick (yes, it *is*
important) with your family, the frozen
Northumberland Strait outside
the window a ghost looking in
while you dine, no doubt,
on leftover turkey and mince,

and I think of Frank's love of the unrequited,
the longing

and invention he needed to articulate his poems,
those windows.

The Adirondacks rise outside my hotel window
into grey light, your chest pushing
against my hand last
week as it slid, a cross-country skier
                                        down and across
the plateau of your stomach, fingers coiling
round your cock in clouds of snow,
my mouth a blizzard about to
                                    touch down, which you
sometimes becalm, afraid (I am not sure)
of my teeth or tongue or what
you may or may not pass on,
the springs of your bed
sighing beneath us, a stand-in
in some menage-à-trois (I said to
make you laugh), though you want this
variation (not the laughter)
hidden from all those who listen.

Something Frank never worried about
in the 50s, the emergencies he meditated in
the midst of (despite McCarthy)
more *automatisé*,
generations of Abstract Expressionists at the Cedar
apprehended by his conversation and surreal
appetite for straight men, Irish
tears and bourbon, jazz,
                                    spontaneous poems
dribbled unrevised
on the backs of coasters in 10 minutes flat

for someone in their circle (the nerve
of those private
asides drawing the rest of us — his future
readers — in) before he headed out
onto 8th Street drunkenly at 2 AM, alone or not alone,
love with a Manhattan skyline a sentimental
disease of his cruisy,
immuno-deficient (i.e. vulnerable) spirit only.

In our time love has become a slogan, a cold
wind howling in the streets
of liberation, something we keep before the courts,
a paper coolly delivered at seminars
worldwide where doctors,
scientists, and activists compete
on how best to shield the sick
and unsick from variations mutating
like wind-sheer in the blood and in the minds
of those who wish us
dead, hate
no less virulent than in Frank's time —
only how the language is used
has mutated,
has kept mutating since his death,
though how it mutates and the aesthetics
of mutation (a.k.a. The Tradition)
allow it, chimera-like, to persist in secrets.

Frankly speaking, as Frank would say, the discourse
from the bathtub should be direct
(hot or cold), i.e. ________,
find me irresistible, though I can be
a klutz, for instance nearly
dropped Frank in at least once so far;
the sodden pages might well have frozen
shut and cut his story short
(which would be sad since he died
(not from love — on Fire Island
a beach taxi ran him down) at 40).

This afternoon the wind has been too
unspeakable and crystalline
for anyone to skate for long on Mirror Lake.
The wind-chilled glass in my window
changes steam rising from the bath
to frost and now I can't see
myself, so am lost and ready to confess
that I, Frank's pale imitation (Bruce says
I echo his looks), wasn't straight

about you with John and Lorraine
this morning over breakfast, invoked you
not in conversation by name
(whom am I protecting?),
only as someone's son who came here once,
not my lover lured by the fleeting
weekend leaves with your parents to stay
in this hotel, perhaps sleeping comfortably
in the roomy bed where last night I dreamt of you,
where you might have once
dreamt about someone like me,

anticipating our bodies, a variation
on the unconscious,
therefore primordial and beloved.
Desire takes many forms, but perhaps what
is unspoken cannot be
edited out and (sweet ellipsis) becomes
the content of the poem —
                                        windows blown out
by winds loosening chance
ecstatic needles from stands of white
pine on some far shore even
a city boy like Frank would walk along
for lack of anything else
new to write about.

ETHER NOTEBOOK

Somewhere, outside my window
    while I dream, you laze beneath the hypnotic
        maples, laze

with Lampman and Scott, dusk
    running warm
        yellow fingers over the braille

of your wind-effaced,
    forgotten marker in Beechwood Cemetery.
        Words no one

cares to read any longer, dates
    and a name, the first
        man to fall to earth in this still

unsettled country,
    a suicide or effaced
        seeker of thrills, the black

hot-air balloon lifting
    above the grounds of the Central
        Canada Exhibition in 1888, you pulled

upward by the handling line
    you loosened
        and would not let go of

unlike the other men who fell
    back from the ascent, the balloon
        skittish

as a prize bull, time
carrying you
high into the blankness

of September, a local
journeyman, your grip blue
knuckled above the disbelieving

and speechless
crowds, the novelty of an escape
from gravity

enough to draw them in, to buy
stereoscopic slides of distant, unfamiliar
flights above

Paris and New York, those nearby
as you rose
dwelling on your parting

words, reported the next day
in *The Ottawa Free Press* and 100 years
later read on

microfilm in the periodicals room
of the public library.
"Thomas Wensley's Awful Flight

Through Space," your final
'good-bye' entered into the record, the ether
of my brain.

*

Thomas Wensley, your goodbye
    final. A suicide or seeker of thrills.
        Huck Finn lighting out for the territories.

Lampman in the crowd
    as you fall, running with the other
        young men outside

the Bank Street gates
    to Holt's field where already dead
        you break upon the ground, the shattered

fact of your body, bones like ship-ribs
    poking through the skin,
        excreta and unspeaking

eyes, your lungs the envelope
    of a balloon torn, voided by rapid
        descent. No more words.

Lampman turning away,
    mystified by your daring
        or despair as gravity broke

your fall, his own foolish
    rheumatic heart weakened
        years later by a lifelong

love of nature, the desire
    to enter by canoe the strenuous
        unwritten text of the boreal, a suicide

or seeker of thrills, dead
    at 37, my age
        even as I dream, Lampman

and Scott pushing up the Gatineau, words
    of the journey transcribed
        from the rocks and leaves, no portage

turned away from, pushing
    the rugged form
        of the iamb, oxygenic

essences spilling
    round the prow, paddles working
        against and into the current's metaphor.

*

How to make
    sense of the senseless?
        Inspiration

rises with a balloon
    and lets go, shatters, lies buried
        with the nation's dead

in Beechwood Cemetery, gravely
    effaced, forgotten for a century until
        someone comes to

live nearby among
        the ephemeral maples
                and begins to dream. Who is this

man who fell to
        earth; who is Lampman?
                Who am I to write these words?

They claim I am
        sleeping, claim that below
                my window Beechwood Cemetery is

crimsoned with leaves,
        that a balloon once passed overhead,
                that a man fell,

that a poet watched this
        descent, learned
                nothing and fell himself.

*

The soil
        in Beechwood Cemetery
                grows black and layered. Death

fascinates me. Its richness
        deepens, lyric and year by year
                born of the journey we take getting there.

I push upstream
        with Lampman and Scott.
                I soar

above the city and let go.
    I resurrect,
        my life black and layered,

the gravity of these words grounding
    my spirit, their panoramic
        overview felt at night rising among the cool

soft-fingered airs,
    the lights below distant
        nebulae toward which we all travel.

Wensley falling
    from somewhere no one else had dared;
        Lampman portaging,

the language centred
    on his back until his heart gave out —
        these words a living

memory of their own journey,
    of inspiration's
        decay and transmutation even as I

dream, maples scattering
    sentient
        leaves on a waiting grave.

WHITE SPACE, STRATHCONA PARK

The earth is brighter than the sky,
you say, a man of few

words who talks with me
through the season's first snow

as I tell you about *Chilly Scenes of Winter,*
the movie and the book, the two of us

walking along the Rideau River toward midnight far
from some unidentified, forgotten

or fictious American city unlike this
one with its restrained Victorian

homes, the fine details I never recognize until
you point them out, not a backdrop

to some self-conscious, now-hazy-
to-me story of jilted love undoing itself,

a character whose past I can no longer
account for, unable to let go

of the snow, of some woman who slipped through
his fingers, his psyche out

in the cold and companionless,
walking a neighbour's black lab, a constant

freeze and thaw, the mercurial snowballs
melting in his hands before he can toss them off,

footage of the dog's finely
etched prose running after nothing,

a man's sense of love and distance
learned from someone, another man, *who?* —

elegant and leafless, the branches catching
snow above our heads, the last unnamable

shade of dusk long ago drained
into the black purity of sky —

most of the above in my head but not
yet spoken as we walk, the river closing

over with ice, pewter still too
delicate to bear

weight, the shifting emphases of language,
the mere nuance

of meaning between us, a season
about to fill

cavities with snow, a storm we are
talking our way into, silence

drifting down around us, the footprints
of language ranging as far

as we wish, a path left across the unbroken
white space of Strathcona Park —

the earth is brighter than the sky —
not telling us (until we turn

back) where we have come from, snow
wind-shaken from the branches, silence

already silting in the footprints,
not telling us until we turn

back (again), lost —
our tracks circling over

themselves or others, clues found
in the snow-lined

mansards of Sandy Hill,
Chilly Scenes of Winter, half-imagined

houses snowily walked into, for once
a sense of direction arrived at

without a compass or Ann Beattie's
or someone else's directions, not telling us

until we turn back (reread hastily turned
pages) that we no longer

have (*white space and figure*)
a way or need ("love,

have I found you?") to know where
we are going.

N/WSW

The heart lives in its remembered water

Erin Mouré

time & the river between us
the river two years wide
our births
by different parents
north & south
banks
of the river
Charleswood & Altadore
the tributary blue spruce
forest
now Edworthy
Park & the floodplain
where the drive-in
was
a windbreak
those aspens you can't help
describing
though you don't want to
or do you
vague yellow-green inscriptions
of light shaken loose

in the narrative

westerlies

I never quite lose the feel for

lemon & sensory, felt

somewhere

along the Ottawa

on this literal bus

grey squirrels flat & bloody as driven

maple leaves

on the roadbed of

Elgin Street

midway through *WSW*

loose

leaves of words &

perfectly bound

rattling storm windows of prairie light

opening in my hands

projections

rolling across the open-air

screen of memory

car window rolled down

mosquitoes & swirling yellow

leaves

transfixed by the wide beam

of the projector

your voice

projecting infinite starlight

no one will pay attention to

Praise be

till the narratives end

you say

& the engines idle

anxious

to join with the galaxy of headlights

drawn into the black

hole

the sex drive

a few minutes north

or south in either direction toward or away from

Memorial & Crowchild

the lit train

on the far side of the river

freighted & heading west

along every river between us

the Bow

your river, mine

disorienting

me growing up on the north bank

the opposite

side of

all rivers anywhere

else now perpetually

south

where you are

descriptive leaves

shaken free of

cryptically

falling

on Jeanne Mance in Montréal

loosed into your poems

where you live now

farther

side of the Ottawa, your city

held tenderly in the

river's

mouth, soft

paws softly pausing

before the sacrificial

kill

river of separation

the tongues

dangerous co-mingling of blood

and memory, current

and shed leaves

our river

this one & the first seen

from the North Hill

words

no less safe anywhere

the Children's Hospital above

Altadore

leaves

read & reddening

lit up in the southern night

the long

absent hospital smoke

stack only

we can imagine now

the human remains not remaining

the rich humus

bonfires of leaves

terrible

joys

burning

though still a child

I have not been admitted

in years

all hospitals where I had my eyes

out

(I was five)

& put back in

bloodshot & burning

don't ask me

why & the way out

to the limits

of vision

distance or otherwise

the blank

blinding white fields smoking

on either

side of the page

levies holding back the dark

river

where the ranchers make

hay of the story

with the circular sweep

of the combines

the equations of love

male & female

factoring separately

letting go of how we live

differently joined

burning

that's good

I can't see my way anyhow

the dense subtext of the city

pure braille

implied in the expanding

grid of streets

the river ignores

a raised relief of sodium streetlights

brief

conjecture

felt from the air

somewhere along the flight path

away from McCall Field

with direction

less navigational aids

words left lingering

far below

on the north bank

along unnamable rivers

chanced upon everywhere behind leaves

bonfires

cigarettes & eyes

burning

under starlit sometimes clouded

infinities, the birth

city of the plains

a terminal of departure

while desires

rise

& fall with the moon

on the west side of the Rockies

pale

gravity of light apprehended

from far off & enticing

the sea

syllables sudden and oblique

tsunami

memories in tumultuous

realignment

& ephemeral, ebbing

backwash, the glittering

lyric swept

clean

RECIPROCITY

This keyboard and these fingers.
The strings and bow of your son's tiny violin.
These words I enter.
This music.
Reciprocity, our friendship, like Canada
strangely bittered and under threat.
I sit before my computer,
these words I enter hours after the solar eclipse.
Weather emerges from memory,
projects itself

in waves of rain that etherize on contact
with the screen I look
through and into, entering a thunderhead
of words, walking down avenues
of darkness and light I can just imagine,
lightning with each keystroke falling
between the trees on the other side.

With my fingers I graphically fail
to reconstruct a country
that, as of today, is missing
one afternoon of sun, a place and time
where already we may no longer live,
two friends, two founding nations,
or so we were led to believe.

We seem to conflict
with each other, the other voices,
Mohawk and Cree, the borders
that may someday eclipse us
so unlike the ones we count on.
Who exists more where (carbon-based or electronic):
the other voices reclaim something
of what once was
theirs — history and the subconscious.

Your son takes up his bow —
this is memory — for the first time
leans into the the long
sweep of each movement, the vibrating
stretch of gut giving us some
thing to talk about until at last we talk
much later — *this is also memory* —
about what long ago we did not say,
which then made room
for silence that was not
silence but the inexpressible,
other voice's quiescent, resonant
like Mozart's variations
re: some star in the carbon
molecules of the brain.

This keyboard and these fingers.
The words they enter.
The scape of the virtual.
Algorithms conjoined like countries.

Lightning, a shadowed windbreak of poplars,
Mozart. Tarte au sucre. Cree.

THROUGH

Or is this just another, but timeless dream?
And can I speak to these whom I have encountered
in that other dimension? How do I seem
to them? Can they see me watching? Do they know I am here?
— Robin Skelton, "Afterwards"

A clearing opens in the forest, not always
at dead centre. Old growth falls back
from thinning air as we hike ever
closer, finding our way between screens of low
branches exhausted of leaves, the emptiness
ahead magnetic, a portal of light whose gleam
is neither dawn nor memory nor dusk. Some halt
at its margins, the light faint and impenetrable
while others ease past, their eyes a murky stream.
Or is this just another, but timeless dream?

Or is the clearing a heart with a hole about
to grow larger, its torn breadth almost
sufficient to absorb your or my absence?
The heart is an ice floe whose edges erode as it
swirls, its hub caving in underfoot as we run
toward or away from whatever void that blurred
over with ice while we were resting at night.
The heart melts within the dimly lit lake of the body,
the reeds slowly emptied of voices and shorebirds.
And can I speak to these whom I have encountered?

Their words escape from our ears, each one
far from its origins, their cadences
forfeiting all pattern, blood-cool, pure,
echos evacuated from a cavern whose ceiling
sweats nitre. Far below we are each in a boat
in the throes of crossing the most extreme
darkness, its opaque waters deaf to the noise
woken by oars as we puzzle a way forward.
Where shall I set anchor? Will I dream
in that other dimension? How do I seem?

We suspect this is the finitude of individual
consciousness, the last intimations
of metaphor fragmentary, the body no longer
able to sum its parts into something like itself.
A forest clearing hollows out a cavern of ice,
a boat melts into a portal of light, and fear
dematerializes so quickly we are through —
phosphor burning the hands of those we abandon.
Could one among us have made this any more clear
to them? Can they see me watching? Do they know I am here?

AQUA POETICA

This river a boundary
crossing boundaries

the Saskatchewan

a moving cell, first memory
dog barking
into bedroom and hand grabbing hold of

early-morning fur washed up
well downstream from wherever, a body

of sound and snow-melt
caught above Angel Falls somehow and the cachement
brimming over, bloody
hopeful (and accidental) spring.

Moving toward and not forward

beyond Batoche
a man with blood like mine,
my mother's blood bearing

reports of

gunfire carried by sandy and wind-crazed
river cliffs to where he stood
sentinel, in 1885, and seeing nothing,

words I hear

in the blood, the photocopied diary
my lover read
aloud
(over my shoulder) in 1990:
"and time lost rounding the bends in the stream."

Moving toward and not forward

beyond the mouth,
phantom

nerves lengthening into salt water and expiring

storyline stirred,

history of the worn-down carried this
far beyond —
Riel and my lover set
adrift and no
longer heard from and not forgotten

Summary evaporation and condensation.

Rain falls.
Thunder and shock therapy of the clouds.

The shortest channel,
the most moving.

Hands apprehending

a tiny river-pilot on his original
night-crossing,
a voyageur about to discover
light: *the word "and"*

intimate conjunction repeated at every

bend in the flow,
my first

recollection of this love of words.

CENTRE OF THE WORLD

CENTRE OF THE WORLD

Flying from Toronto to New York, Lake Ontario contained
below in its bed like a heart, the Niagara River
feeding the fall's vaporous
roar louder than the Pratt & Whitney engines,
the propeller-blur transparent as the water
churned up high above
the cataract, the dangerous rainbows lowered
over each passenger on deck, the *Maid of the Mist* rocking
too achingly close to the rocks, the distant call
of the Saint Lawrence already in the gills of the fish
hurled over the edge,
that mighty aorta sweeping them and a thousand
misguided freighters into icebergs
clogging the Labrador Current, the immortal whir
of the *Spirit of St. Louis* hanging frozen
over St John's at twilight
for nearly 70 years, Lindbergh Paris-bound,
the slightest elegiac
breeze eastward greased with the lonesome
ambitious hush of his engine,
Magie unable to shake the wintry feel
of him leaving New York,
passing like an angel of death
over the remote province of her birth while she waits
for my plane to land, a reunion
downtown at Moonstruck over cheesecake
where 23rd meets 9th,
and I remember you,
several stations north on the Broadway line,
lying on the floor by my bed 10 years ago

10 floors up above Morningside Park, its dark heat fallen
moonlight between Harlem and Columbia,
that fortress on the Heights
where I lived 6 months, your body naked
and loud as gunfire,
mine explosive as ice beneath loose-fitting sheets
and somehow one of us taking
the other's hand,
our fingers quick darts of light and shadow
shamelessly confused, the glow
off your body backlit
by landing lights caught in a final haloed
approach to LaGuardia
by the uncurtained square of darkness above my bed
as you climbed in beside me, took my cock
into your mouth like I had let no other man,
held it so gently
inside, nuzzling me, nuzzling me long after I came,
1983, the centre of the world,
The New York Times ignoring something untoward leaking
into and through the blood,
men sitting behind tables heavy with pamphlets,
wanting the truth told near Sheridan Square,
Magie no doubt at 7th and Grove
with a petition long
before we met and me refusing the pen,
turning away from a strange man
at the corner who might now be dead, who pointed out
the bar where it all began
or came to a head,
those riotous queers throwing their garters and more
at the NYPD, our ladies of the barricade,

14 years before we lay
together without a protection
we could not have conceived a reason for,
lay together and for me the first time without fear,
in New York City where I had come to be
the poet I am
and instead became the lover of men I had always been,
the roar of Niagara
at last swamping my heart, the Seaway traffic,
Lake Ontario and all its sunken wrecks and sleek long
distance swimmers engorging my veins,
the blur of propellers,
the blur
of years passing and your body and the landing lights,
the runway still guiding me into New York
and Charlie Lindbergh, why did he leave for Paris
like all the others before and after,
the transatlantic crossing and fame
as beguiling as sex,
why didn't he
turn back with his good looks and extra fuel,
give up on flying solo, that sad denial
of life, maybe he is
still up there
since 1927, waiting to land, Paris struck
from history's flightplan, engine
singing as we circle
round for the final descent, wheels down
on Friday, September 17th, 7 years before 2000,
the feast day of any saint I want,
so get this coffin into the terminal and let me rise
out of my window seat,

buy St. Lindy a drink on Christopher Street
in your name, sweet anonymous man,
my cock still tingling
with the soft fur of your upper lip,
the rhubarb curl of your tongue;
may others dock in the harbour of your mouth
as I did, to pull away
from the moorings affirmed and longing for romance,
Staten Island ferries all of us,
the city lights rising out of the grey midnight rain,
lost maids of the mist searching
every tributary, the four chambers of the heart
full and moody like those lakes
far inland, Lake Michigan hanging tumescent
between the tanned, corn-silk thighs of the Midwest
while over a drained cup of coffee
near the blunt tip of Manhattan Magie prays
to St. Veronica
in a language slowly freed of the virus,
which the virus has made, and though I had not known it,
flying out of my precambrian remoteness
into New York, this is what I have
come to live for,
words no longer protected by mute grief, at last
sounded fluidly and exchanged,
which I relish the taste of
and repeat for you, wherever you are,
their etymology musk-scented and epistemological,
a heartbeat murmuring transmutation,
revolution and praise,
asking Veronica not to lift from one more face
another likeness of the bloody shroud

she once tore from a passion-weary Christ,
Who needs the relics, Ronnie,
a candle lit
for each one of us, the living and the dead,
Magie's ladies of the centre,
of the world, aflame
on her makeshift altar of twinkle-lights
and crystals, history undoing itself in Chelsea,
Never forget, she says, *life is sacred,*
makes all things happen.

CENTRE OF THE WORLD

for Sarah Binks

Far from the cities, where fields
  of No. 1 Northern
    once shone golden in the tempest,
      coriander and dill rise,

a floodwater spreading over the plains.
  Farmers part the still
    winds of the TSE's ruined futures,
      the fallen

world price for wheat
  like Moses while children
    of the death star
      generation

cultivate signals under the eaves
  of clapboard houses
    outside Odessa or on reserves,
      the centre

of the world, small hearts
  like jerry-rigged satellite dishes pivoting
    this way
      or that, blood veins

dedicated and busy
as ditches at sunset, the hinterland
in reverse,
less likely to be

far beyond the fall-out
of revolution.
They are the big
bang themselves, at last

their poetry, at last
some sweet songstress of
Saskatchewan, wherever he or she is,
makes things

happen. They have names
for themselves rooted outside
the barbed-wire fences of space/time,
up- and download them

from dreams sparkling with dust
rising off back roads near Paradise Hill,
hazy from the pulsing
smoggy lights of the Ginza.

Names less likely to silt under the chill
soils of prehistory
where cowboys and maiden
aunts who taught

school lie buried in abandoned
churchyards or somewhere
on the range. No one will plough
them under, these children

unearthing arrowheads and buffalo skulls,
the remains of what
is said could not survive Darwin.
The marrow in their bones

is binary, is
charged with the celestial
noise of fenugreek
and their switched-on modems.

CENTRE OF THE WORLD

The heart wobbling in its orbit.
The Cambrian sea
circulating unconsciously through the body,

its rich nutrients dating us
the early fishes
still feeding among

the porous

sponges of our dreams.
Arteries harden

in the brain as the planet ages,
amnesiac
and anxious about the future.

5.5 billion by 1994.
5.5 billion more by 2050.

Everyone of us isolated inside the body,
the centre of the world,

hearts overcrowded

and hungering for shelter, the bounty
of the sea unstable
and exhausted, imagination less

likely to be caught and glistening

in our global nets.
Refugees meet by chance

on a Toronto subway platform,
nostalgic
for countries that abandoned them without mercy,
the heart dangerous and sentimental

because there is no going back,
subway trains jangling

as they circulate beyond Bloor and Yonge,
a cacophony
of conflicted nerves.

In Cairo delegates meet,
the sixth UN Conference on Population,
one week in the news,

the centre of the world,
the history
of our time a succession of cardiac
arrests, the failure

to love, orphans wandering
in Rwanda, ethnic
cleansing in Bosnia, Haitians capsized
and drowning off the Florida coast.

There is no room anywhere,
the four chambers

of the heart shutting down one by one,
the delegates
in disagreement, news reports

circulating around the world

electronically and through the body,
the blood-brain
barrier uncentred, overrun

by AIDS, famine, war,
what is left
of the food supply stored in the flesh of those

who can put something aside
for tomorrow, flounder
and sole
cooling in the freezer overnight, complicity

filtered out by the kidneys
and discarded.

We are on life support
now
and time is

running, is running out,
the freedom
of movement between countries less
important now than the flow

of goods.
To give birth or not

a matter of ethics or economics

not of the heart, vestige of the ancient

body of water that long ago
contained us,
all of us single-cell
and unselfconscious lifeforms that evolved.

Schizophrenia.
Mitosis.
The delegates all over the map,

unable to decide on anything except
what divides us,
though borders are still

contested, refugees stateless
and the spirit
starved for love without conditions,

the centre of the world
homeless and always moving. Oblivion crossing

frontiers by osmosis. The blood.

Bad conscience
familiar and predatory as protozoa.

What's a soul to do?

The heart
wobbling in its orbit.

CENTRE OF THE WORLD

A slim volume of poems waiting
on a bookshelf.
                    A coincidence.
Elizabeth Smart, aged 23, in Better Books

on Charing Cross Road in late August 1937,
out of the rain and browsing,
looking for something

to read that afternoon at Harrod's idly
over tea, a colonial
restless for life at the centre

of the world to remake her,
insatiable blue

eyes devouring the dust jacket, conjuring
the author from his
use of the language, not the man
she would later meet with his wife in Big Sur,

but the poet she would make him into,
the equal of his own words,
the father of her four children,

alchemy in the middle
of a busy shop, one among many

not far from the station, the other
browsers looking for something more useful
than poetry, something to fill

an empty hour spent in a rail car,
George Barker no more
important to them than destiny, unaware

of the young woman standing transfixed
in the aisle, her body
aching to give way to passion, blond hair aureoled

against a window as the sun broke through
briefly, a poet open in her hands,
her whole life leading up to this moment,

his words, how they would change both
of them, she knew it, the words
changing
as she set them to heart.

The shop clerk, if he remembered her,
saying he merely sold the young woman a book.

To tell you all this

happens unexpectedly, courage found
while we sit,
swept up in the inevitable

conflagration of rain, heat amassing
all morning,
the sky opening, sudden

incandescence and thunder,
the Great Hall
of the National Gallery, its lightning-shot
glass chrysalis providing us

shelter as we overlook the river
in Ottawa,
city of Elizabeth's birth.

Scribbling entries in her diary

for each day's work in the garden,
the kitchen table gilded
with a watery
twilight about to leave her

cottage outside London,
porch door
ajar and luminous against the dark —

her squandered riches

not unforgiven, the books
she found no time
to write
not quite overshadowing the few

she did, loving a man
followed
from continent to continent, a man
hopelessly disinclined to help

raise children who remained
for her
the risk and consummation
of her artistry and womanhood,

a kind of bloodline
of words
born of the body — such a solace

the last years of her life —
language from the beginning

a vitalizing obsession,
despite the judgements
of others and the solitude.

Elizabeth writing down

what she remembered,
the pantheism of nature,
the Gatineau Hills, the sibilant

wind-shaken maples scaling the cliffs
toward the Library of Parliament,

the same agonized trees turning
crimson as we speak, the apprehension
of summer chilled and beautiful in the recurrent

fallen leaves.

The glass table between us — clouds caught
looking up through us while we eat,
our transparency,

the centre of the world,

the crowds — thunder's aftershock —
echoing about us,
moving through history
as they move through the galleries,

ascend and descend through rain-dazzled
light, water-soft
balustrades between floors polished
by elbows and lingering hands,

our history added to lovingly,

no one aware of us talking,
our intimacy
effortless and screened by the collective

memory and amnesia of the nation
shaping us, its passion
and white noise housed under one roof.

Art matters for some reason
and we sit joined

by the coincidence of a good friend
mutually known, whom I have not talked with
in years, who long ago hoped

for some reason you'd have
occasion to meet me,
words you forgot and remembered

and responded to,

my book chanced upon and open
in your hands, a man

undone page by page, face peering

up from the dust jacket,
eyes with no sense

of the future, temporarily
blinded by the advent
of middle age and the camera flash,

a slim volume of poems waiting

in some Kitsilano bookshop you escaped into,
out of the rain overtaking
Vancouver, a man not yet known

to me with hazel eyes irresistible
and love-worn, fingers
with bitten nails holding the book open,
lips measuring the words

under your breath, looking for something

to read the world by,
language to make us feel less alone.

Your letter arriving last Friday,
the same day as your plane,

a coincidence,

your invitation to lunch coming out of nowhere
for both of us, a surprise
slipped in
to an envelope with your poems and a photograph.

Walking to the Gallery we paused
before the elegant
brick house on Daly Avenue —

its gardens tangling with leaves —
where Elizabeth capriciously lived out
part of her girlhood, chrysalis

for passion
and the courage to make words.

The solitude of the writing desk,
the agonized possibilities

through language
for connection, for joy —

Elizabeth's legacy, though I never
understood this till now,
light descending
in rash fragments about us,
our eyes meeting between paroxysms of thunder,

our tongues discovering laughter
and an endless
downpour of words she would revel in

and bless —
whatever happens,

whatever promise our bodies
hold for us in warm
and knowing arms, the realization come to us
suddenly about coincidence

and destiny,
how fiercely they possess us.

CENTRE OF THE WORLD

What hills we make for ourselves.
Lilienthal,
Otto.
Killed in the midst of the great experiment, his glider

pulled from the sky
by the force
at the centre of the world, the body's core — *the force* —

years of inspiration crafting
endless

pairs of wings, the first tentative
set those of adolescence,
each wing
three fanciful metres long, gilded

not with wax but goose

down, Otto securing

(with Gustav) all the feathers to be
found in Anklam, in Pomerania,
in the 1860s, testing
his "senseless

whims" at night, away from schoolyard
jeers, wanting to spread artificial wings above the medieval

town in the alchemic
privacy
of moonlight.

Wilbur Wright said gravity

was Otto's motor.
The gravity of desire

felt deep down and to anyone
else unexplainable, sudden insight lifting

him, light

and aerodynamic
as the bones of the storks he so admired,
Vogelflug als Grundlage der Fliegekunst,
published in 1889,
a lifetime

of observation lifting him from his garden,
then from the Rhinow Hills,
his will mature and unflappable, the movement

of his wings not important,
Otto not
a bird but soaring like one, expansive

wings relaxed as the stretched

arms of a dancer "in the flow /
of wind currents floating, the rapture to know"

carrying him far — *two hundred* metres, *three hundred, four,*

such poetry the intuitive dynamics
of lift and drag as he steered
with his body,
an acrobat shifting the centre

of gravity, balancing among the continual

agitations of the wind, risking
to look
away from the doubtful

countenance of the planet and the gathering crowds,

Lilienthal often rising above

his elevated

point of departure, the constant
grassy slope he climbed
to get this far

falling away as he quickly rose — persistent, unspoken

longings buoyed by the supporting
power of the air
offering

him "a correct view of the landscape,"
when at last he would turn back
to look,

the questioning

eyes of fame far below,
the air under his fixed wings

freeing him from anxiety with soft
music, "like that
of an Aeolian harp," which the breezes tricked
from the wires of his glider,

the quiet earth between his knees,
the limits
of the horizon pushed back.

What hills we make for ourselves.
Outside Berlin,
fifteen metres high, raised by men, and lonely: Otto's hill.

It was not technique that killed him.
It was not his hill.
August 19, 1896.
He simply fell from the sky,
pulled to earth by gravity, his motor.

"Sacrifices must be made," his final words.

And his epitaph,
the words of Leonardo:

The great artificial bird will some day
set out upon its first flight
from the summit of a hill.

Those who observed him would navigate

higher into the mysteries of
what makes
things stable.

What hills we make for ourselves.
Aspiration.
Artifice.
The centre of the world.

NOTES ON THE POEMS

Confidential takes its inspiration, in part, from news coverage of the Commission of Inquiry on the Blood System in Canada, which was presided over by Justice Horace Krever. The report of his findngs was published in December 1997.

Homoeroticism resulted from a close reading of Dr. Richard A. Isay's *Being Homosexual: Gay Men and Their Development* (Farrar, Straus and Giroux, 1988). In this book, the author proposes a model for gay-male psychodynamics to guide analysts and others in an affirming, sympathetic treatment of their gay male patients.

From a Journey Around the World was inspired by *First Impressions: European Views of the Nature of Canada*, an exhibit curated by Victoria Dickenson at the National Library of Canada in 1993. The artifacts on display included the frontispiece to Aleksandr Filppovich Postels' *Illustrationes Agarum*, which was published in St Petersburg in 1840. A copy is held by the library of the New York Botanical Garden in the Bronx.

Centre of the World (Otto Lilienthal) was written in response to Petra Halkes' *Dream of Flight*, a painting in the collection of the National Aviation Museum in Ottawa. Lilienthal's own (translated) words in the body of the poem, which are indicated with double quotation marks, were attributed to him by Robert Kronfeld in *Kronfeld on Gliding and Soaring: the story of motorless human flight* (John Hamilton, 1932). The English-language title of Otto and Gustav Lilienthal's *Vogelflug als Grundlage der Fliegekunst* is *Birdflight as the Basis of Aviation*.

ACKNOWLEDGEMENTS

I would like to thank the editors of the following magazines and anthologies where many of these poems were published or are forthcoming:

Acta Victoriana: Destiny, Loosestrife
The American Voice (Louisville): Destinations, Leaving the Map
The Canadian Forum: Home Movies, New Technology, Reciprocity
The Capilano Review: Undercurrent, Dementia, Number Theory, Mississippi, Saranac Lake Variation
Contemporary Verse 2: Centre of the World (Elizabeth Smart)
Dandelion: The Bit Like Desire
Everyman's Journal: Dementia
The Fiddlehead: Pushing Upstream
Hook & Ladder: 18 Degrees North
James White Review (Minneapolis): Loosestrife, Wolves
The Malahat Review: Chicken Boy
Missing Jacket: Lake Huron Variations
modern words (San Francisco): Destiny
Other Voices: Objectivity
Our Lives (New York): Dementia, Mississippi, Undercurrent
paperplates: Autopsy
Poetry Canada Review: Beyond Recognition, From a Journey Around the World
The Prairie Journal of Canadian Literature: N/WSW
Prism International: White Space, Strathcona Park
Queen's Quarterly: Bloodstream, The Crisis of Lyricism
Somewhere Across the Border (www.letelier.com): Aqua Poetica, Reciprocity
TickleAce: Centre of the World (Sarah Binks)

"Destinations, Leaving the Map," "From a Journey Around the World," "Autopsy," "Chicken Boy," and "Saranac Lake Variation" were collected into the limited edition chapbook *Destinations, Leaving the Map* (Ottawa: above/ground press, 1995). "Tantrum" was anthologized in *Vintages 94* (Quarry Press, 1995), and was reprinted in *A Room at the Heart of Things* (Véhicule Press, 1998). "Undercurrent" was reprinted in *Siolence* (Quarry Press, 1998). "Saranac Lake Variation," "Dementia" and "Beyond Recognition" were reprinted in *Written on the Body* (Insomniac Press, 1998).

"Objectivity" is dedicated to Alison Beaumont, "Chicken Boy" to Owen Fairbairn, "Lake Huron Variations" to Philip Robert, "From a Journey Around the World" to Victoria Dickenson, "Night of the Blue Moon" to Sandra Nicholls, "Through" to Sylvia, Alison and Brigid Skelton, and "Saranac Lake Variation" to _______.

These poems were written within earshot (or telephone- and/or modem-range) of many friends whom I obliged to hear/read countless drafts, especially Maria Stewart (wherever you are), Philip Robert, Bill Ralston, Jim Gurley, Neile Graham, magie dominic, Nadine McInnis, Sandra Nicholls, Blaine Marchand, Norma Lundberg, and Helen Humphreys. Without these patient, sometimes abused ears, I would have been howling — however sensitively — into the vortex. I am also grateful to the Municipality of Ottawa-Carleton for a 1994 "A" Grant that permitted me to work on this book, if not at my leisure then according to the dictates of my skittish inspiration. Thanks also goes to David Rimmer for having a comfortable chair across from his desk at After Stonewall Books. Except for height, he and the Friendly Giant have a lot in common. Thanks also to Erin Mouré for her example and the permission her work en*genders*, and for her postcard of Jean Cocteau and Jean Marais. And thanks to Michael Holmes for his faith in this book; to depart slightly from a line of Phyllis Webb's, you "threw a bridge of value to believe." And lastly, thanks to Robert Gore for feeding me in Vancouver and for hinting it might be time to stop writing for awhile and go for a walk by the ocean.